LYRICS OF LIFE.

—BY—

JOHN GROSVENOR WILSON.

NEW YORK:

CAXTON BOOK CONCERN, LIMITED.

1886.

TO LILLAH.

Dearest, to thee I dedicate the fruit
Of loving labor all inspired by thee,
Thine were the hands that planted at the root,
To thee belongs the blossom of the tree.
If haply men find some small portion sweet,
Worthy to hold their hearts a little space,
Then will the task be not all incomplete,
And my delight will be to see thy face
Smile with unselfish joy, and my regret
That in such weak, imperfect song as mine
Scant meed of praise can come to thee—and yet
I could not fashion thee a worthy shrine,
Nor yield thee full, fair honor tho' my pen
Thrilled with all power known to gods and men.

CONTENTS.

Lyrics of Life.

AN AMERICAN ODE.

IN the very blackest night
Toiled the peoples, worn and weary;
Blind, they sought the healing light,
Bowed beneath a burden dreary—
When a gallant seaman sailed
Forth, in search of lands unhailed.

Hope and Courage rigged his spars,
  Genius winged him for the quest,
New-born science of the stars
  Led him ever straightly west,
  Till, before all eyes intent,
  Lo, the new-found Continent!

Then the human rivers rolled,
  Some in gladness, some in tears,
Puritans of sternest mould,
  High-born brilliant cavaliers,
  Filled with valiant deep unrest—
  Flower of England's sturdiest.

Frenchmen waved their oriflamme,
  Stately Señors sailed from Spain,

Sober men of Amsterdam
    Swelled the universal strain,—
    "Shores redeemed from isolation
    Be the cradle of a Nation!"

Years of childhood come and go,
    Lo, the lusty, youthful giant
Feels the blood of manhood glow,
    Leaps erect with shout defiant!
    Vague delight the peoples stirred—
    Kings and priests affrighted heard—

Heard the guns of Lexington!
    Heard the cannons' deadly roar!
Many moons waxed full and shone
    Crimson in the blaze of war.

On the virgin continent
Freedom pitched her ample tent;

Called, and waved her snowy wand,
Open flew the airy portals—
Ah! the plains that stretched beyond,
Canaan for all toiling mortals;
Sweet the summons, clear the voice,
"Happy world, rejoice, rejoice!"

Swiftly speed the pregnant years,
Comes the virile age of steam,
Axes bright of pioneers
Through the falling forests gleam—
Ever westward with the sun
Still the human rivers run.

From the German Fatherland,
    From the Green Isle's mournful dales,
From the Scandinavian strand,
    From Italia's ancient vales,
    Haste they to the larger life
    Eager for the splendid strife.

But a sudden, sombre shock
    Makes the very heavens rattle!
Freedom's symbols reel and rock
    In the whirlwind of the battle!
    Vague affright the peoples stirred—
    Kings and priests delighted heard—

Heard the guns of Sumter boom!
    Heard the vows of peace derided!

War's huge death's-head through the gloom
Grinned upon a land divided—
Life in death, or death in life,
O Republic, thine the strife!

But the last sad fight is fought,
Freedom still maintains her sway,
Southern valor goes for naught,
Yet—O rapture!—strange to say—
They, the vanquished, from defeat
Pluck the fruits of victory sweet.

For in wild Atlantic breeze
See the blowing banners curled!
By the far Pacific seas,
Mark the blended stars unfurled!

While between, a giant band,
Mighty States clasp hand in hand.

Hand in hand, in union blent,
Making one great royal Nation!
Single as the firmament,
Set supreme in sovereign station!
Law's upholder! Freedom's home!
Of the world the glorious dome!

On Republic! strive, nor pause,
Freedom guard in all thy lands,
Such as seek to wreck thy laws
Crush with thy majestic hands—
And thy future thou shalt find
Bright with hope for all mankind.

RECONCILIATION.

O VOICE of the people, now thunder
For brotherly love;
O freemen, forever tread under
Your hate, rise above
The promptings of greed and of malice,
Declare to the world,—
"Behold we have drained the red chalice
And down it is hurled!"

O victors, cry out to the conquered,—
"The fight has been fought,
The Union is safe and fast anchored,
Fair Freedom is wrought,
And, brother, the old love is strengthened,
Thy blood is our own,
Together our days shall be lengthened,
And peace shall be known."

Hark, hark, from the Southland the murmur
Of Industry's horde;
The hammer and plow they grasp firmer
Than ever the sword;
See! white men and black men as neighbors,
All lending a hand,
As Hercules toiled at his labors,
Transforming the land.

And South winds, and winds of Atlantic,
And winds of the West,
Blow only one flag, one gigantic
Free flag that is blest;
Its stars are the stars of the morning,
Its stripes are the rays
That herald the day that is dawning—
The sun that shall blaze.

DECORATION DAY.

WHERE marbles and mounds lie together
On hillside and dale,
The glow of the bright, breezy weather
Folds all in a veil
Of sunshine and sweet summer gladness,
Undimmed by the rain,
Unknown of the shadow of sadness,
The pallor of pain.

The voice of the wind, as it passes,
    Makes musical hum;
But hark! through the rustle of grasses
    The beat of the drum—
A sob, and a low voice that trembles,
    A down-drooping head,
The morning of Maytime dissembles,
    We meet by the dead.

We meet where the captains of cannon
    Lie under the trees
With those that flew banner and pennon
    O'er rivers and seas,
We stand by the graves of our brothers,
    O valorous host!
On some lie the laurels, on others
    The willows are crost.

But all are as one in their ending,
    No sound of the strife
Comes up from the dust that is blending
    To fashion the life
Of grasses, and sweet-scented briers,
    And deep-tinted blooms
That burn out their delicate fires
    By numberless tombs.

The maiden who mourns for her lover,
    Or friend for his friend,
Learns here that the battles are over,
    That this is the end;
And mothers, who meet in their weeping,
    With quivering mouth
Ask not if their sons that are sleeping
    Came Northward or South.

O gracious and glorified hours!
    We gather to-day
To girdle and garland with flowers
    Our Blue and our Gray;
We kneel by the green graves that blend us
    In brotherly peace,
To pray that affection attend us,
    That hatred may cease.

CHICAGO.

ON the shore of the Monarch of Lakes
Rise column, and dome, and spire,
And the light of the morning breaks
On the City of Wind and Fire!
With the speed of the wind uprisen,
With the strength of fire she stands,
And her fingers of iron imprison
The wealth of a world in her hands.

In her towers and turrets of stone
She is strong, and her walls of brick—
Yet her resolute builders have known
The day when the flame rolled thick,
When fled as a dream was her glory
And round her the smoke-clouds curled,
And with wonder and weeping her story
Was writ in the heart of the world.

But the tokens and treasures of love
Came to her from all mankind,
With the smoke of the wrack yet above
They came, and the self-same wind
That rolled the fire over her beauty
Blew message of comfort and light,
And she rose from the dust to her duty,
Renewed and refreshed for the fight.

They are gone, the dark days of despair,
  She is bright in her new-born fame,
And she filleth the wide world's air
  With the glory and growth of her name.
About her the great States cluster,
  That breathe in her nostrils life,
That clothe her with joy and luster
  And strength for the giant strife.

Lo, from street, and from crowded mart,
  The music of progress rings,
And her citizens, great of heart,
  Are of commerce the lords and kings;
O, from her no years shall dissever
  The well-won crown of the West,
For the light that endureth forever
  Upon her doth rise and rest.

1883.

SIR PHILIP.

ONE morn the prairie reached afar,
A sea of golden harvest fields,
It was the hour when twilight yields
Her misty mail of moon and star.

Light rosy clouds sailed far away,
The dewy corn just faintly stirred,
And here and there some waking bird
Piped out his little roundelay.

Adown the level country road
A gentle wind did scarcely blow,
And all was very still, when lo,
Came Philip with his market-load.

He eyed the farm-house o'er and o'er,
And thought of her who slept within:
From such light chance doth love begin,
Haply forever to endure.

And as he rubbed his sunburnt brow
The imp that round each lover flits,
To warm his heart and fire his wits,
Said slily,—"Let her hear you now."

Beneath her window did he stand,
Gallant as errant knight of old,
Though on his breast there gleamed no gold,
Nor lance nor sabre in his hand.

He sang an old familiar song,
Of simple words and simple strain,
Half-sad, half-glad the low refrain,
Perchance the notes were something wrong;

He heard her window softly slide,
He saw her sleep-bewildered eyes,
He caught her look of shy surprise,
Her gesture marked with pretty pride,

And off he ran. The kindling morn
Lit more and more the laughing land.
Small happy breezes hand-in-hand
Went chattering o'er the billowy corn.

Ah, ever blooms the old romance,
In wood, or wild, or western plain,
As under stately groves of Spain,
Or in the sunny fields of France.

O Youth and Love! O Love and Youth!
Twin suns that light the wastes of Time!
You put to blush the cynic's rhyme,
You are the sweet eternal truth.

MIDWINTER.

ICICLES hang
Where Summer sang,
The north-winds clang
From frozen lands;
O'er hill and valley,
Down wind-swept alley,
The storm-clouds sally
In whirling bands.

Farm-house and field,
Alike concealed,
Beneath the shield
Of Winter lie;
The world, snow-sheete.,
As one defeated,
A queen unseated,
Makes mournful cry.

The short day dies,
No stars arise
In serried skies
That shake with snow,
The rough wind whistles
And hurls his missiles
Where keen ice bristles
On rocks below.

On rocks that reach
Above the beach,
Where sit and screech
        The gulls at night,
By waves foam-fretted,
With sea-weed netted,
Their sharp teeth whetted
        For dark sea-fight.

But winds may roll
O'er sound and shoal,
And cheek by jowl
        The storm-kings ride,
Men meet together,
Despite the weather,
Though fierce flakes feather
        The roaring tide.

In happy homes,
When darkness gloams,
The beaker foams,
        The feast is laid,
Bright fires are lighted,
Sweet troths are plighted,
Fond hearts united
        Of youth and maid.

And on lone heights
The beacon-lights
Burn bright o' nights
        For ships at sea,
Though warring Winter
May smite and splinter,
Or ice-peaks glint, or
        The snows fall free.

BALLAD OF LOVE'S GRIEF.

A MAIDEN sits with idle ball and skein,
The clock's long pendulum swings to and fro,
The blazoned light of day grows dim with rain,
With rain that turns to sleet, and sleet to snow;
But still she sits and watches, singing low,
Her voice as clear as birds' when dawn appears,
"Dearest, why break your vows and leave me so?
The smiles of Love are fewer than the tears."

A mother kneels with tortured heart and brain,
She hears her baby's breath come hard and slow,
And, bending, clasps the wasted face again,
The little lips make piteous dumb-show
And all is over—save the useless woe,
The mother's plaint that some sad listener hears,—
"Ah, little life, flown fast that I may know
The smiles of Love are fewer than the tears."

An old dame looketh thro' the window-pane
To where the village churchyard sleeps below ;
Alone, she croons a half-forgotten strain
That, as in dreams, recalls the long-ago;
A dreary song, that makes the salt drops flow,
That rouses memory, dead to hopes or fears,
"Ah, life thro' which the bitter breezes blow,
The smiles of Love are fewer than the tears."

ENVOY.

Day springs from night, from mold the roses
grow,
From hearts of fire are formed the tranquil
spheres,
Therefore put trust in recompense, although
The smiles of Love are fewer than the tears.

DANCE OF THE FAIRIES.

WHO are these that gather in the green moonshine
Round the sleeping rose-tree and the rose-tree vine,
By the folden lily and the scarlet bloom,
Frightening the cuckoo in the leafy gloom?
See, they dance, dance, dance,
And the trance
Of a wild enchantment creepeth
O'er the rose-tree as it sleepeth,
And they sway, sway, sway;
For the day is far away,
For the night is not yet over,
And each flying fairy lover
Hears the ringing joyous measure
As he dances, dances, dances,

Thinking,—"What is life but pleasure
And a happy lover's fancies?"

And the green leaves bending with the tripping feet
Hear the far-off answer ringing clear and sweet,
Water-fays are dancing on the singing waves,
Merry elves are dancing in the green sea-caves;
See, they dance, dance, dance,
And the glance
Of the moon upon them falleth,
Thro' the wreathing spray she calleth
And they sway, sway, sway;
But they hear her voice and listen,
And they shimmer and they glisten
In the splendor of the spray
As they dance, dance, dance,
To the music of the kobold
Who from out his den has hobbled,
With a sea-shell at his mouth,

And a wind from off the south,
He is blowing, blowing, blowing,
And the summer-night is going,
But they dance, dance, dance, dance,
Dance it away.

From the forest flitting out the elfin bands
Meet the sea-fays dancing on the moon-lit sands,
Joining hands they revel thro' the joyous night
In the green light of the moon and the faint starlight;
See, they dance, dance, dance,
And the lance
Of the red star breaks upon them
And the dew is shining on them
As they sway, sway, sway;
Careless now of whence or whither,
Skipping hither, skipping thither,
In the night that soon must wither,
Die, and fade away.

APOLLO AND DAPHNE.

EVE o'er the sacred vale—in joyous mood
Apollo, fresh from war with Python, trod
The flowery sward, and from his shoulder slid
The quiver, and the bow fell from his hand,
Whereat he seized his silver lyre and sang
Of Love, the lord and god of gods and men.

So journeying, he marked where Daphne lay
Hot from the chase—her sandals laid aside
From the bright-veined, small, slender, supple
feet;
Her tunic opened to the welcome wind
That softly stirred the folds and half-displayed
The lilies and the roses of her breast
Immaculate—thus lay she, aimlessly
Twisting her golden hair about her head,

So perfect-sweet that, struck with swift desire,
The god made straight toward her, saying
fast:
"O love, thy love is more than victory!
I lay my crown of conquest at thy feet—
Thy name shall tremble on my harp until
Olympus' gates are closed!"

But as the fawn
Starts and takes flight at baying of the hounds,
So Daphne ran, her lithe limbs fleet with
fear—
Sandalless, yet incredibly swift she fled,
And he pursued—but, mortal, none could
match
Apollo's speed—till, panting, worn, she sank
Beside the stream Peneus, silver-waved,
And called to him who dwelt therein: "O
thou,
My father, shield me from Apollo's love!"
For lo, the god stretched eager arms to her.

He leaned above her, that his eyes might take
Foreknowledge, and he laughed right lordlily—
But as he gazed she paled and shrank, and
seemed
A thing of mist—the river flung fierce foam
Upon her—from the thickets flew the birds
And hovered o'er her, motionless and mute.
Then from the mist, the cloud, upon the sward,
Tall, slender, stretching heavenward, uprose
A tree unlike all others, and the god
Groaned as he knew the maiden changed and
lost.

And from the river rose a solemn voice,
Hollow, as is the murmur of a shell:
"O thou, who hast won glory for all time,
Fixed and eternal as the changeless stars,
Hast thou not learned that love is not to
force?
Love is a shadow's shadow—love is fine
As Summer wind, and subtle as the film

Spun by a spider on a rose's thorns,
That hands can scarcely touch, or eyes behold.
Wield thou the warrior's sword, strike harp
of song,
But rest content with these—relinquish love
To hearts that yearn, that thirst for naught
beside,
Content to watch in humbleness, to spend
Immortal years in wooing."

So the voice
Spake, and Apollo moaned disconsolate,
Casting his arms in vain about the tree.
A low wind smote the leaves and stirred
the boughs
To plaintive rustlings, and the red sun set,
Wherefore the sky was dim, till scattered
stars
Made light, and winged-foot Mercury leapt
forth,
Pointing his wand across the silent world.

SONG OF THE WIND.

FROM the far frozen
Plains, that are closen
Ever, and chosen
        Only of snow-clouds,
From that waste war land
Known as the Nor'land,
Round the bleak foreland
        Ride I the low clouds.

Fleet as the hour
Speed is my dower,
I am the power
    The spirit of motion;
Hark! the beginning!
Space for the winning!
All with me spinning,
    Earth, island, and ocean.

Ho, for the journey!
Clang, O ye horny
Peaks! the wild tourney
    Of tempests unravel,
Who then shall bind me,
Bruise me, or blind me,
Yea, or shall find me,
    As tireless I travel?

Where the wave flashes,
Where the spray dashes,
Where the sea clashes
    Her cymbals, foam-hidden,
Filled with the moonlight,
Thrilled with the noon-light,
Winter and June light,
    Roam I unchidden.

When the thick-lying
Forests are sighing,
Through the boughs flying
    I bear their assurance
Out to the arid
Sands that have tarried,
Harassed and harried,
    Worn wan with endurance.

When the skies thunder,
Riven asunder,
Rush I on under
    The lightning's long arrows,
Howling and hurling,
Cracking and curling,
Whistling and whirling
    Down rivers and narrows.

Then, the storm ended,
Rain and earth blended,
Lo, unattended,
    In Summer's sweet season
I slip down some alley,
Or wild woodland valley
Where red robins rally
    To wrangle and reason.

Or with low whirring
Speed I unerring,
Tenderly stirring
    The leaves of green covers,
To blend in my flying
With vows and denying
And amorous sighing
    Of light-hearted lovers.

THE LEGEND OF VINETA.

(From the Drama of "Nordeck.")

O CITY sunk forever,
Vineta!—yet of thee
The spectre glows and glistens
Above the foamy sea.

Wherefore thy doom was spoken
No mortal tongue can tell,
But from thy grave of billows
Thy phantom weaves a spell.

For if on thee, together,
A youth and maiden gaze,
Their fates are twined forever,
Howe'er may trend their ways.

Eftsoons they love, but sorrow
Pursues their hearts' sad quest,
Unless again, together,
On thee their eyes may rest.

Then rise once more, Vineta!
Appear to those that wait!
And Love, made lord and master,
Shall break the bonds of Fate.

THE GRAND SALUTE.

TWO hundred busy years ago,
One morn in sweet September,
As fair and fresh a day did blow
As any can remember.

The town of Kelderheif was filled
With merry noise and bustle,
Nor whirr of work nor hum of guild
Was heard in all the rustle.

For to the town a mighty man—
The Duke of Bragabenna—
Was coming, by the road that ran
From far-away Vienna.

Up rode his shining cavalcade
    With nodding plumes and tassels,
And priest and baron, man and maid,
    Were each and all his vassals.

The city gates swung open wide,
    And, as the Duke rode under,
The guns that stood on either side
    Roared out their greeting thunder.

So gay the town, the Duke rose up,
    And in his stirrups standing,—
"Now bring," said he, "a brimming cup
    While this we are commanding.

"Each Michaelmas, come sun or rain,
    In honor of our visit,
The same salute shall fire again,
    And, that ye shall not miss it,

"A fund for this I here provide,
A fund to last forever!"
He drained the cup and, laughing, cried,—
"I'll be forgotten never!"

Ah, happy hope of many men,
What would ye do without it?
Ye toilers of the sword and pen
Who daily dream about it;

Who sigh for fame, who die for fame,
And after all what is it?
The roaring of a ducal name
Upon a ducal visit.

Two hundred busy years have fled—
And now the quaint old city
Drones out its life, unsung, unsaid,
Save in some random ditty.

The whirling wheels of modern life
Roll on the distant highway,
The famous road of Kelderheif
Is but a pleasant by-way.

But every year come Michaelmas
Awakes an ancient gunner,
In crimson cap and bright cuirass
Arrayed in martial manner.

With stately mien the loud salute
He fires across the meadows,
The daws stop pecking at the fruit
And gain the oak-tree shadows.

The grazing cattle roll their eyes
In drowsy meditation,
The gray-haired shepherd coughs, and cries,
"Ah, what a noisy nation!"

Till in the Autumn haze the smoke
    Grows every moment thinner,
And flitting from the friendly oak
    The daws resume their dinner.

TO A BABY.

O LITTLE stranger, lately come
From out the misty region,
Now speak, before your head shall hum
With science and religion,
And tell us whence and what you are,
And how we all appear—
Don't roll your eyes and stare afar,
Pretending not to hear.

You lie so still, and roll your eyes,
Perhaps you were forbidden
To talk at all, you look so wise
That something must be hidden;
Come, baby, let the secrets out
That all the world would know,
And quell at once the winds of doubt
That round about us blow.

A rumor runneth far and fast
As to our constitution,
That from an unknown protoplast
We've grown by evolution;
Now, baby dear, if you would do
A service to your race,
Say what is false and what is true—
And don't contort your face.

There—now you are at peace again.
    No doubt you were astounded
To find a world of grown-up men
    Half-witted and confounded.
You look so solemn—Ah, perchance
    Some other tongue you speak,
Conned over in eternal trance,
    More fluent than the Greek.

A language born of singing stars'
    Melodious communion
In space serene, where nothing mars
    The peace and perfect union;
Ah, baby dear, if strains so sweet
    Yet echo in your ears
'Twere best if Time were not so fleet
    In counting up your years.

For you will fret, and fume, and fuss,
Grow lean, or haply fatten,
And be just like the rest of us
With all your lore forgotten.
Come, tell us of the mysteries.
You listen, but are dumb,
You will but roll your elfin eyes
And suck your dainty thumb.

IN ROSAMOND'S BOWER.

SHE.

A PLEASANT noon
Of flowered June,
In sweet attune
    All forest sounds,
Pray, sir, a boon,
Weave us a rune
While last night's moon
    Still flies the hounds.

HE.

When ladies pray
Men must obey,
There is no "nay"
    To ladies' prayers,
So have your way,
We'll sing to-day
A mournful lay
    Of old affairs.

SHE.

Yon moon last night
Was filled with light,
Now wan and white
    She runs her journey,
As faded quite
In all men's sight
As storied knight
    Of tilt or tourney.

HE.

So all things fade
In Time's gray shade,
This very glade
    Hath seen the day
When, half-afraid,
With silken aid,
To woo a maid
    A King found way.

Ah, frail and fond
Fair Rosamond!
You spun a bond
    For royal lover;
A silken wand
It wound beyond
Thro' ferny frond
    Of copse and cover.

Forgotten e'en
The jealous Queen
When you did lean
    With whispered greeting;
The leafy screen
Took on a sheen
Like rose-lights seen
    At fairy meeting.

Alas, alas!
Such days must pass;
Fate holds the glass
    That runs for lovers,
Swift to harass
As winds that mass
From swampy grass
    Where poison hovers.

Fate, cold and gray,
Did Love betray—
By Love's own way
    The Queen sped thither,
With lips to say
Despair, dismay,
With hands to slay
    And eyes to wither.

Revenge she bore
To Love's sweet core,
And all was o'er
    And Death was sated—
O Eleanor!
O fierce and frore!
Forevermore
    Of all men hated.

But thou shalt reign,
O fair one slain!—
Nor false disdain
    Shall keep thee lowly,
Nor aught remain
Of shame or stain,
With perfect pain
    Of love made holy.

SHE.

A tangled knot,
A mournful lot;
I had forgot
    This tale illicit—
The air grows hot,
We'll leave this spot,
My hand, sir—what!
    You dare to kiss it?

JARL ERIC'S DAUGHTER.

ON Finland's waste and windy shore
Jarl Eric built a castle,
And reared a massive Hall of War,
Great oaken ship-beams for its floor,
Huge rafters to ring back the roar
Of mighty midnight wassail.

No woman ever entered there
Save Eric's only daughter,
Sweet Gyda of the golden hair;

Men sang her praises everywhere;
Her eyes were bluer than the rare
Deep blue of south-sea-water.

And often when the dawn would creep
O'er dim unfinished revel,
Jarl Eric, nodding, half-asleep,
Would mutter,—"She shall never weep,
No man shall have her soul to keep
An' be he god or devil."

It chanced, one windy winter day,
Jarl Eric from his doorway
Looked seaward thro' the foam and spray
And saw the clear cold sunlight play
On seven ships in line array
That flew the flag of Norway.

He looked and frowned, but did not see
    His daughter stand beside him,
Until she cried,—"It is for me
That Harald sails so fearlessly;
He comes to ask my hand of thee!"
    Quoth Eric,—"Woe betide him!"

In vain she wept, in vain she plead,
    He would but answer always,—
"I swore a vow thou shouldst not wed."—
The ships wore round the harbor-head,—
"Chain up the bridge!"—Jarl Eric said,—
    "Cross-bar the gates and hallways!"

From every ship that shoreward drew
    A hundred men were landed;
Then Harald on his war-horn blew

A blast that shook the morning dew,
Afar the startled sea-gulls flew,
And wind and echo blended.

"I come for Gyda," Harald cried,
"Jarl Eric, she doth love me!"
Quoth Eric,—"An' to win your bride
Ye needs must lord it far and wide
Over my castle's pith and pride,
By all the gods above me!"

They stormed the walls till day was dead
And came the midnight hour,
The watch-fires flared a fiery red
That made the sky burn overhead
When Gyda from her chamber fled
And climbed the castle-tower.

No moon above the sea did hang,
    But stars she counted seven;
Below, the horns of battle sang,
And battle-axe on armor rang,
And shield met shield with clash and clang
    That shook the arch of heaven.

When Harald saw her standing there
    He cried,—"No walls shall hide thee!
O sweet my love, so passing fair,
The brightness of thy golden hair
Shall make each jutting stone a stair
    Until I stand beside thee!"

Then up he climbed the sheer ascent
    By stones and ledges narrow,
Jarl Eric watched him as he went,

And all stood still in wonderment
And on their battle-axes leant
    Nor shot the whizzing arrow.

A thousand times he seemed to fall,
    But, looking up to Gyda,
He held his way, they heard her call,
As, leaping o'er the topmost wall,
He caught her hand, and, straight and tall,
    Stood merrily beside her.

Quoth Eric,—"He hath won her fair,
    He lords it o'er the castle;
God bless her gleaming golden hair,
Nor may it whiten o'er with care;
My broken vow must needs beware
    Of mighty marriage wassail."

TWO RONDELS.

1.

MARC ANTONY.

AFAR the trumpets blow,
They call,—"To arms! to arms!"
Ah me, I cannot go,
She holds me with strange charms.

I hear the shrill alarms—
Her hands are white as snow—
Afar the trumpets blow,
They call,—"To arms! to arms!"

Her speech is soft and slow,
Her kiss my cold mouth warms,

Her eyes with languor glow—
  And so it be, what harms?
Afar the trumpets blow,
  They call,—"To arms, to arms!"

2.

COEUR-DE-LION.

Sound, sound, a battle-charge!
  Blow, horn; and beat, O drum!
For see, along the marge
  The Moslem banners come.

Hark! hark! the mighty hum—
  Yon crescent groweth large—
  Sound, sound, a battle-charge!
Blow, horn; and beat, O drum!

Shout,—"Richard and Saint George!"
 Shout! shout! and strike 'em dumb!
Crash battle-axe thro' targe
 Till fright their hearts benumb—,
Sound, sound, a battle-charge!
 Blow, horn; and beat, O drum!

CIRCE.

I MARVEL at thy beauty, love, thy white
Satin-smooth skin, thy exquisite round breast,
Thy rose-red lips, that mine so oft have prest
Faint with the strong delight.

I gaze into thy gray, perplexing eyes,
Dilated now with consciousness of me,
Within their depths, far, far, within, I see
Riotous forms arise.

I whisper "Helen," and the fields of Troy
Glitter before me with their shielded throng
Of men that fight and make eternal song
For one fair woman's joy.

I murmur "Hero," and the waves below
Leap at the sound, as if again they bore
Him that for one sweet kiss left light and shore
To tempt the tide's dark flow.

And Phryne's name slips like a soft caress
Thro' my enchanted brain; I see again
That grave assemblage of gray-bearded men
Stunned at sheer loveliness.

These are thyself, and yet to thee are thrall,
For love was never known till thou wert born;
I dreamt of it, till thou didst come one morn,—
Therewith I knew it all.

Knew, and inhaled the perfume of thy mouth,
O subtler scent than of all roses slain!
That fell on me as an abundant rain
Falls on the fervent south.

Knew, and made fast my hands about thy
waist,
And felt my bright blood beat from feet
to brow,
And kissed thee in the throat, as I do now,
As thus with thee enlaced.

Turn, if thou wilt, still will I look at thee;
If thou dost hide thy face, I watch thy hair
Twist at my breath into a golden snare
That doth entangle me.

O kiss me into silence! shall I sing
When thou art here to drink my life
away?—
O fire of Love! gone are the night and
day,
Forgotten everything!

THE POET TO THE PHILISTINE.

THE creature of a thousand moods
That lift him to the highest heights
Or plunge him to the deepest deeps,
He lives his life, awakes, and sleeps,
Is jocund now with thee, or broods
Alone, while flesh with spirit fights.

Thou deemest him a crazy loon,
Thy daughters hold him pitiful;

What room in the rude roar of life,
The clash of trade and party strife,
For his wild ballad to the moon
Or rhyme of lovers mythical?

Knight dauntless he in Freedom's lists
With fiery lance of eloquence;
In clear and clarion voice he calls,
And waits for answer—on him falls
Thy smiling sneer at theorists,
Thy scorn of callow innocence.

When with free hand he scatters wide
Such coin as comes to minstrelsy,
Sweet laughter lieth in his eye,—
In holy horror thou dost cry,—
"Spendthrift!"—but O, thou wear'st with pride
Thy warm, sleek suit of usury.

A ring of fire, a ring of ice,
The cruel chaplet binds his head;
Thou thinkest to defray thy debt
To him with laurel leaves, and yet
His gentle art will not suffice
To earn for him his daily bread.

But O, poor dullard, clogged with gold,
His life to thine is king to slave,
The bright blood bounding in his veins
Would rack thy heart with aches and pains,
The mysteries to him unrolled
Would drive thee, shrinking, to thy grave.

For he, as Homer, calls to life
Heroes and gods, a deathless band;
As Dante, delves for truth in dream;
As Shakspeare, finds the force supreme;

As Goethe, calms eternal strife;
  As Hugo, leads to love his land.

He hears the song that sings the sea,
  He trills a duo with the lark,
  He listens to the sonorous chant
  Of peaks with storm made resonant;
Thou thinkest all is still, but he
  With keener instinct crieth,—"Hark!"

For him the myriad flowers bloom
  With brighter hues and sweeter scent
  Than for another; for him rise
  New constellations in the skies—
Where thou perceivest only gloom
  He scans a radiant firmament.

He maketh virtue beautiful,
    With beauty charms and conquers vice;
    Thou canst not understand, nor know
    Why God hath made his like—for, lo,
His song the grief of hell can lull
    And make more joy in Paradise.

A Modern Benedick.

A Modern Benedick.

PROLOGUE.

O DREARY discussion of marriage and money!
O useless debate of self-evident truth!
Certain it is that the milk and the honey
Of life are the guerdon of bachelor youth.

I am quite satisfied—just five-and-twenty,
Modestly making a station in life;
Fond of society, pleasure, and plenty—
How would it be if I took me a wife?

O venomous visions of butchers and bakers!—
O fearful forebodings of milliners' bills!—

Rather at once would I join with the
Shakers,
Vowed and devoted and shielded from ills.

Heaven be praised that endowed me with
reason!
I smile at the ravings of poets and
fools;
Never a girl shall convict me of treason
To these, my judicious and sensible rules.

Old folks may maunder of days departed
When youths went courting of shy sweet
maids,
Now we but flirt in a gay, light-hearted
Fashion, and only a dunce upbraids.

O, I am armed! and from Cupid's quiver
Never an arrow on me shall fall;
Why, the mere thought of it makes me
shiver—
But I must be off to the Charity Ball.

I.

THE FIRST MEETING.

IS this I, the unbeliever?
Is the ball still going on?
Or am I my own deceiver,
Shall I find myself anon?

Thro' the charming mimic thunder
Of the strains of *William Tell*—
O, the rapture! O, the wonder!—
Rang her low voice like a bell.

And I looked—it seemed for hours—
She was standing by a vase
Filled with rare and splendid flowers
That enframed her flower-like face.

Underneath her eye-brows even
  Shot a glance that fell on me,
And the ball-room was a Heaven,
  William Tell a jubilee.

Vain my maxims! Vain resistance!—
  O, her eyes, that smile and shine!—
Will she keep me at a distance?
  Dare I think to call her mine?

II.

THE LOVE-LETTER.

"LOVE me little, love me long"
 Ran the ancient poet's rhyme;
Tame the thought that bred the song,
 Love, my darling, knows not time.

Love me, wilt thou, for a year?
 I will seek no more than this,
Centuries of hope and fear
 Can be counted in a kiss.

If thou wilt not, then, O sweet,
 Love me for a single season,
In some flowery far retreat
 Lost to sight or sound or reason.

Ah, too much I ask of thee,
  Love me, dearest, for a week;
Seven days, wherein to be
  Lord of joy—but speak, love, speak;

For a moment, then, as fleet
  As the flight of light above me,
Time for hands and lips to meet—
  Ah, but, darling, love me, love me!

III.

ACCEPTED.

WAS the wide world cold to thee, love?
Did the starry skies seem cold?
Why, the winter world to me, love,
Burnt bright with the flame of old.

But I wandered with thee mute, love,
For fear in my heart was strong
That hopeless would be my suit, love,
But, darling, I read thee wrong.

For the hand I held and kissed, love,
Was trembling with love for me,
And a sudden rose-red mist, love,
Rolled over the land and sea.

Thro' the mist's red heart a light, love,
    Struck swift from the dawn-touched skies,
But to me more sweet, more bright, love,
    Were the shadows of thine eyes.

IV.

ABSENCE.

I STOOD in the night, and I envied the stars,
For my love was away, and I stood all alone,
But the stars could shine on her, the glorified stars,
And I hated them for it, as gayly they shone.

Then the wind came,—the wind had blown soft by my love,
Had kissed her and fled from her, fled to tell me,—
And I trembled with rage, but still from above
Shone the stars, and the wind blew along to the sea.

V.

THE ENGAGEMENT RING.

GOLDEN little emblem
Of a holy vow,
Glitter, gleam, and sparkle
In the sunlight now,
Round her slender finger
Clasp your tiny band,
Why, you look so yellow
On so white a hand.

Golden little prophet,
    Telling of the time
When the moon of marriage
    Up the sky shall climb,
When austere December,
    Clad in mail of rime,
Shall with merry music
    Ring a wedding-chime.

Yes, it means, my darling,
    We shall thro' the years
Know our joys together,
    Mingle all our tears;
Joy will be more joyous
    That I am with thee,
Sorrow lose its sadness
    That thou art with me.

Hold your dainty finger
   Where the ring may shine,
I can scarce believe, love,
   You and it are mine;
Silent, and so happy,
   At your feet I kneel,
Clasp your hands in mine, love,
   Heart to heart reveal.

VI.

COURTSHIP DAYS.

WHEN leafy Spring with grasses green
The whole wide world doth cover,
I whisper to my love,—"I ween
No fairer days will e'er be seen
For suit of happy lover."

When golden Summer sits her throne,
The flowers' fairy mother,
My love and I walk all alone,—
"Ah me, such days were never known,"
We say to one another.

When pleasant Fall with winds from west
Blows hazes thro' the weather,
My love and I, with laugh and jest,
Are sure these days are far the best
We ever spent together.

When whistling Winter's horns do wind,
And Summer streams are frozen,
My love and I are of one mind,
The very coldest days, we find,
Are just for lovers chosen.

VII.

MARRIAGE-EVE.

THE light of your eyes, my darling,
Is a beacon bright for me,
As true as any light-house light
That burns along the sea.

The sound of your voice, my darling,
Is sweet as that sweet strain
That floated, the first Christmas-night,
Above Judea's plain.

And you unto me forever
Shall be as that fixed star
That guideth home all mariners
From rolling seas afar.

VIII.

MARRIAGE MORNING.

TO-DAY, to-day, to-day,
O ring, sweet bells!
Ring, but you cannot voice my full-fledged joy.
All night I watched to catch the first faint gray
That in the east foretells
Latona's boy.

Orion, all too slow,
With unsheathed sword
Threaded the glittering mazes of his march;
The moon reluctant lingered, loth to go
Across the starry ford
From arch to arch.

But, clothed with light and flame,
Day leaped above,
As a vast Victor who rebellion quells;
All space rang vibrant with my darling's name,
For lo, her name is Love--
O ring, sweet bells!

EPILOGUE.

THE light of morn was o'er the land,
When graciously you gave your hand
To me—ah, happy, happy day!
I knew you could not answer nay
To such a loving, sweet demand.

Fortune may dwindle or expand,
Now frowning dark, now smiling bland,
Yet in your eyes there shines alway
The light of morn.

Betimes with grief or care unmanned,
I come to you, and ne'er withstand
    Your smile, that brooks no dull delay—
    Ah, love, though we are growing gray,
Still shines for us, on hill and strand,
        The light of morn.

Echoes of Eld.

Echoes of Eld.

EXCALIBUR.

"THOU art here, the Lord's Anointed,
King of men and knight of heaven,
To the trust thou art appointed,
Unto thee the sword is given;
As a sign for thee, a token
That the light again is breaking
Thro' the gloom of time unspoken
To the dawn and to the waking.

"When the fields of heaven sounded
With the roar and shout of battle,
And the whirling spears rebounded
From the shields with ring and rattle,
This the sword that Michael wielded
With a fire and strength supernal,
Till the rebel hosts, unshielded,
Fled from light to night eternal.

"Strong as Michael shalt thou fight them,
They that bow before the idols,
And the blazing sword shall smite them
From the horses and the bridles;
Yea, the heathen, stunned with terror,
Shall behold the blade advancing,
With the flame that burneth error
From the hilt and jewels glancing.

"Lo, the weary world is weeping
In the toil of her transgression
For the justice that is sleeping,
For the wrong and the oppression,
For the nights that quake and quiver,
For the days that dawn in thunder,
For the years that shrink and shiver
At the shame and at the wonder.

"But the guilty shalt thou scatter,
And the sword will bravely brighten
As the standards sink and shatter,
And the foeman's face shall whiten
At the sound and at the glitter
Of the brand above him flashing,
Till the death-shriek, shrill and bitter,
Drown the din of armor clashing.

"So thy kingdom shall be founded,
And by justice thou shalt hold it,
And its fame shall be unbounded
As the wide seas that enfold it;
And the harvest hailing hither
Shall encamp on all the acres,
And the noxious weeds shall wither
As the sea-foam on the breakers.

"Till the right grown wrong with surfeit
Shall uprise and challenge proudly,
Then the peace shall all be forfeit,
And the trumpet-call sound loudly;
Then the sword shall rouse the thunder,
And the echoes will awaken
All along the sea, and under,
Where the mermaid rides the kraken.

"For the cycle will be ended,
And shall come the desolation,
And the close shall be attended
With a noise of devastation;
And the ruin will be utter,
For the foe shall overmaster,
And the royal flag shall flutter
To defeat and to disaster.

"When from out the nether regions,
With a mighty thunder-rattle,
Ride the clanging, shouting legions
Of the storm and of the battle,
Then the solemn doom shall follow,
And the King shall bow before it;
When the great sword striketh hollow,
To the giver then restore it."

SIR PALAMIDES.

SIR PALAMIDES, Saracen,
Right worshipful among the men
Of Arthur's days, rode thro' the fen.

Till, past the skirts of fen and wood,
On lonely Humber's bank he stood,
Grateful for that sad solitude.

And looking, aimless, east and west,
Bemoaned his love and beat his breast,
And yearned to end his ceaseless quest.

When up the stream in silence sped
A royal barge, and huge and red
Grinned at the prow a wyvern's head.

Red silk swept o'er the deck, and made
A stately couch, whereon was laid
The body of a King, arrayed

In robes of state, and in the hand
It held a scroll, and to the land
The barge drave fast and keeled the sand.

Sir Palamides leaped on deck,—
"Alack!" quoth he, "a royal wreck!"
And touched the crescent at his neck,

Unrolled the scroll, and this it said—
"Hermancè, of the City Red,
Father and King, here lieth dead.

"Murdered by him he loved the best.
Good knight, to set his soul at rest,
Pray sail the river on his quest."

Then swore the knight, upon his knees,
To sail the quest, and with the breeze
He set the prow toward the seas.

Adown long Humber swift he sailed,
Anon some castle-warder hailed,
Or knight that rode full-armed and mailed.

He sailed into the open sea,
And still the wind blew fair and free.
"I marvel at this quest," quoth he.

But seaward yet the vessel bore,
Until an island rose before,
And straight the barge drave to the shore.

People that watched there to him spake,—
"Thou seekest Helius, for whose sake
Our King's good heart did bleed and break.

"For lo, our King was kind and mild,
But very old, nor blessed with child,
Wherefore he sought this monster wild,

"Made him as if he were his own;
But he so longed to sit the throne
He killed the King, and we made moan;

"He and his knights then mocked and said,—
'Bring forth the royal barge of red
And set it sailing with the dead.'

"The which we did, but slipt within
His hand the scroll that told the sin,
And now, please God, the right shall win."

"Yea," said the knight, "an' if God please:"
Addressed himself, and cried,—"Let these
Base knights come now; I take no ease

"Until I lay them low in dust
And hang their armor up to rust.
God and the Prophet shield the just!"

Then Helius and his knights were wroth,
And seizing arms they hurtled forth
As when the wind blows from the north.

Many they were, and woful strong;
They fought the Saracen so long,
It seemed that right would yield to wrong.

The people watching made great dole,
And wept with pity for his soul,
And shades of night began to roll.

Till, with a thrust clear thro' the head,
The Saracen smote Helius dead;
And who were left in terror fled.

Uprose great shouts of joy, and all,
With banners, marching from the wall
Of the Red City, loud did call,

And hail him King: whereat the knight
Spake thus,—"That I have won the fight
I praise God's grace, not mine own might.

"But as for me—alas, I needs
Must wander on among the weeds,
That haply I may yet do deeds

"Of honor fair, and ease my heart,
Wear out the pain, and dull the smart,
Wherefore, good friends, I must depart."

Then, stepping in a barget gray,
Sir Palamides went his way,
And sighed for Isolt, night and day.

MORGAIN.

I.

THE QUESTING.

OUT spake the King,—"My sister's hand
I give to any in the land
Who brings her back to me."
And forth they rode in quest of her,
Heart hot with hope, each plied the spur
To win such high degree.

By yellow fields of harvest-corn,
Thro' cities old and weather-worn,
Down road and winding lane,

By shallow ford and river-bridge,
Along the rugged mountain-ridge,
They rode the quest in vain.

They rode, it seemed, across the world,
They saw the flags of Summer furled,
They felt the dead leaves fall;
The trees grew naked by the way,
And from his ramparts, bleak and gray,
They heard the Winter call.

Once on a misty moorland waste
They slackened in their headlong haste
To bury one that fell;
Then on they went, but grew afraid
To die and have no ghostly aid,
Nor mass, nor passing bell.

And from that day the frozen sun
Ne'er dawned but that they lost some one
Of their undaunted band;
But still they never backward turned,
And still the strong desire burned
To win the Princess' hand.

Till one alone was left to climb
The weary way; the biting rime
Had dulled his armor bright;
At last his horse fell under him,
Then, chanting low a lover's hymn,
He perished in the night.

The night wore on, and very soon
Uprose the white and waning moon
With her thin train of stars;

Withered she was, and very old,
And all the stars were blue with cold,
And shaken, as from wars.

And when the winds of Summer blew
Along the road, and flowers grew,
And fell the Summer rain,
They found them lying in the dust,
Their armor rotted thro' with rust,—
They rode the quest in vain.

An errant minstrel wandered down
To where, within the royal town,
The King sat on his throne;
Therewith he learned his knights were dead:
"Let mass be sung for them," he said,
"And carve their names in stone."

But when the sister of the King
Heard all the royal church-bells ring,
        And knew the knights were dead,
She came from out her hiding-place
And painted red her laughing face—
        "The news are good," she said.

II.

THE MARRIAGE.

But still the royal church-bells rang,
And still the monks their requiem sang,
        And over all the land
A shadow fell as of despair,
For none were left with heart to dare
        The quest of Morgain's hand.

But lo! a murmur, growing loud,—
A strange knight parts the curious crowd,
His step is firm and free,
Tho' he has journeyed from the land
Whose yellow belt of shining sand
Dips in the endless sea.

"God grant," said he, "I be not late."
He stopped before the palace-gate
And wound his silvern horn;
The gates of Merlin opened wide,
The church-bells ceased, and as a bride
Uprose the ruddy morn.

Forthwith he spake unto the King,—
"My liege, let all your church-bells ring,
And make a marriage-chime."

With roses wreathed about her head
The Princess came, and this she said,—
    "It is the foretold time."

Even so he claimed the Princess' hand
And broke the spell; throughout the land
    Died down dark dismal fears;
And they that rode the fruitless quest
Lay quiet in their graves, at rest,
    Mourned for with maidens' tears.

But where *they* rode, that wedded twain,
Thro' whirl of wind and rout of rain,
    Toward the endless sea—
What quest was theirs? What woman's wile
Lay lurking in the faint sweet smile
    That masked her reverie?

They rode unto their journey's end,
The Lonely Land where meet and blend
The sea-waves and the shore—
He left her in her bridal-room
Alone.—Night wove her garb of gloom,
Earth shivered to the core.

She watched—the moon, a very skull,
Floated upon the sea-rim, dull
The scant stars gleamed above;
Then Morgain laughed, then Morgain cried,—
"O, dying moon! O, happy bride!
To live, to laugh, to love!"

III.

THE BURIAL.

Time fled—he heard the Princess say,—

"O knight of mine, the weary way
Is passed, the path is straight,
Lo, thou art mine, and I am fair,
Live, laugh, and love, nor wile nor snare
Can keep one from his fate."

Whereat he fled in shame and fear,
But always did he think to hear
Her voice, and see her face,
And feel her red lips kiss and cling,
Till world and sky did reel and ring
With memory of her grace.

Nathless he came to her again—
She said,—"Be thou the lord of men,
Yet shall thy proud heart bend;

With weak white hands I hold thee mine,
Thy thread of life shall twist and twine
With mine unto the end."

Shamefaced and hot, he held her fast,
Cried,—"Fling the future to the past!
Thy eyes burn fiercely bright."
Soft blew the summer wind along,
A fieldfare trilled his evening song,
And day lay wound with night.

So Morgain wrought a pure knight's fate;
Upon him full the heavy weight
Of sins and sorrows done:
She watched him, ever at her side,
Wax wan and worn and hollow-eyed,
She whispered,—"I have won."

But lo, she clutched him in the night—
With bloodless face, and lips all white,
She cried,—"My time is fled!
Hark! they that rode the fruitless quest
Are riding now!"—and on his breast,
Shrieking, she fell—struck dead.

Thereafter came the royal hearse,
But none would bless; a muttered curse
Greeted the funeral-day;
The moon uprist, so white and lean
That scarce her shadow could be seen
Across the graveyard-way.

By the green grave he stood, and said,—
"O Death, with Love corruption spread,
For nothing lies before."

Even as he spake the earth grew gray,
The endless sea stretched far away
In quest of unknown shore.

SIR BORIS.

AS DANK a night as ever man had seen
On field and town and sullen sea-coast lay,
The waning moon, maligned with mist, looked green,
The ship-lights flickered feebly from the bay,
And all was still, save where, with head aslant,
The white owl croaked his melancholy chant.

It was a night when fairies hied them home,
Their kirtles wet, and clinging at the knee,
And eerie elves from caverns forth did roam
With one-eyed dwarfs who kept them company,
If haply they might meet with some poor wight
And fill his head with visions of the night.

Townward Sir Boris held his joyful way,
The mist hung on his hair, his eyes were wet,
And, as he passed along, one heard him say,
As in a dream,—"My little Margaret;"—
And on his finger shone a single gem
Rarer than aught in the King's diadem.

Onward he pressed, hard by the town he
came,
When suddenly a low, sweet, clear voice
cried,—
"Sir Boris!"—Marvelling thus to hear his
name,
The knight reined horse, and, standing
at his side,
Beheld a fair young girl, with naked feet,
And long hair golden as Sicilian wheat.

She stood as in a hollow of the mist
That curled away and from her breathing
shrank;
Her eyes, more violet than the amethyst,
Shot lovely light; adown o'er breast and
flank
Streamed the remorseless mantle of her hair,
But left her arms uplifted, white and bare.

Elsewhere the mist was heavy, fold on fold
It wrapped around the owlets in their nest;
Sir Boris shivered, smitten with the cold,
Wherefore the maiden clasped him to her breast,
And, grateful for the warmth, he closed his eyes,
While soft she sang to him of Paradise.

She watched his sleep with eyes intent and glad,
And from his finger drew the precious stone;
Sir Boris started, and as one gone mad
Ran for the town—but, nevermore alone,
Behind him danced the maiden, and did sing,—
"See how the mists to Mistress Moon do cling."

* * * * * * * * * *

Meantime fair Margaret slept, and in a dream
Dreamed of her knight and how he won the gem,
When suddenly through that sweet sleep a scream
Rang, and a strong voice loudly shrieked her name;
"Surely," she said, "it was a dream," and yet
Again the voice, now faint, cried, "Margaret!"

And all was hushed—arisen from her bed
In chaste, cold fear, that shook her like a bride,
She crossed the room with swift, uncertain tread,
And flung the lattice-window open wide—
Only the mist she saw, that seemed to writhe
In sickly serpent shapes, alert and lithe.

Nor of that night could any watcher say
    If from the coast a girl sang or a bell
Tolled for a good man's soul—if from the bay
    The ship-lights flickered or the flames of
        hell—
    But nevermore on night or fine or wet
    Hastened Sir Boris to his Margaret.

BALLAD OF SIR LAUNCELOT.

"RIDING the quest of the Grail alone,
Guinevere, Guinevere, pity me!
All thro' the day and the night I moan,
Yearning to catch but a glimpse of thee.
Tho' I make halt by the wan west sea,
Seeking a sign in the high God's name,
Lo, as I tremble and bow the knee,
Gleameth thy face with the eyes aflame!

"Me have I scourged till the blood hath flown,
    Weeping hot tears of misery;
Still thro' the day and the night I moan,
    Yearning to catch but a glimpse of thee.—
Yea, have I striven and sought to flee,
    Ever and ever the same—the same—
Blinding my soul with sweet rarity,
    Gleameth thy face with the eyes aflame!

"Sleeping, I dreamed that the Grail was shown,
    Marvellous bright with clemency;
Waking, I lay on the chancel-stone—
    Ah, but I yearned for the touch of thee!—
Tho' I may bow and make piteous plea
    Unto the Christ and our Holy Dame,
Sweeter by far than all visions be,
    Gleameth thy face with the eyes aflame."

ENVOY.

Guinevere maketh a day of glee,—
    "Who is it cometh to join our game?"—
"Launcelot rideth with bridle free,
    Gleameth thy face with the eyes aflame!"

ISOLT AT THE TOMB OF TRISTRAM.

"HERE, with my arms curled round the sacred cross
That in white warning stands above his bones,
I crouch, with hot limbs pressed against the stones,
And moan his name, and wail and weep his loss.

"Stand back, good sirs—ye shall not drag me hence;
But, pray ye, keep between me and King Mark;
My husband? yes—God pity me—but hark,
Surely ye know not his most foul offence.

"Yet know ye how he came, that rainy day,
When Tristram played the harp to me, to keep
The hours in joyance.—Ah, sirs, could ye sleep,
And in a dream but hear Sir Tristram play—

"How like the tinkle of a silver bell
The sweet notes from his cunning fingers tripped,
In airy melody that softly slipped
Into the heart, with sunny stir and swell.—

"In very heaven of joy I heard him play,
And saw his eyes with love grow masterful;
When, at a sudden, stealthy, noiseless pull,
The curtains parted and for Mark made way.

"I felt my lips were frozen in a smile,
And with that fixèd smile I watched King Mark
Drive his sharp glaive thro' Tristram's throat, till stark
My Tristram lay—and I said naught the while,

"Until that man came to me--half in fear,
I wot—whereat I shrieked, and in a swoon
Fell down, and knew no more until the moon
Rose yesternight, and then I hurried here.

"Now shall Mark come to judge me?—he?—who knew
All of my Tristram's love from first to last,
And knowing how that love would bind him fast
Made use of him to keep his kingdom true.

"Has any man who profits by a sin,
In ways direct or indirect, a right
To sit as judge of what is black or white,
Or join his voice to the accusing din?

"O, I can say no more!—do what ye will!
My heart grows sick above my Tristram's tomb—
O loyal love, how fares it in the gloom?
Dost hear my voice? hath it the old-time thrill?

"Rest, rest, my love—I grow so weak and faint,
Thou shalt not wait me long. O blessed hour!
When from the gate of heaven's portal-tower
Thou wilt rush forth to still my cold complaint."

THE DEATH OF GUINEVERE.

AT ALMESBURY the lights are low—
With muffled step the Sisters go,
And come, and go, in tears, for lo,

With crucifix held o'er her head,
The Abbess-Queen lies on her bed,
Soon to be gathered with the dead.

They deem her holy; she hath taught
How hope may come and faith be bought,
But now she thinks—and this the thought:

"To die. O God! what breadth of doom
Awaits me in the ghostly gloom
That stretcheth out beyond the tomb?

"To die—to die—to go where I
May meet with Arthur passing by?
I cannot die—I cannot die!

"I whisper to myself his name,
I count the years, I count the shame,
And feel the torture of the flame.

"I loved him not, yet well I know
I took his life—and deep and slow
I wrought the wound, I dealt the blow.

"I know not where his body lies—
I dare not meet his clear, large eyes,
Bright with the light of Paradise.

"Why, they would cut me thro' and thro'
Like yonder star, that from the blue
Dissevers this clear drop of dew.

"O Christ! a little time, I pray,
Yet let me live—perchance some day
I may not fear to tread the way.

"Cease, cease, vain prayer—I am grown old.
The thin white hair that once was gold,
The sunken cheeks, half-gray, half-cold,

"The shrivelled breast, the sightless eye,
All wan and worn—they mutely cry,—
''Tis time to die! 'tis time to die!'

"O, I am old and changed! and what
If I should meet with Launcelot
And he should pass and know me not?

"Methinks my heart would throb and swell
Until it broke again—ah well,
'Twould make of heaven a twofold hell.

"To think that we two souls had met
And he had passed, with quiet face set
Away from me, so old—and yet

"It was not love for him I felt;
No love in me hath ever dwelt
Save love of self. Why, I have knelt

"And prayed to God for grace for *me*,
Have moaned and prayed for strength to see
Some hope in gray eternity.

"And in my prayer no name has mixt
With mine, lest it should come betwixt
My thoughts and God's, and leave unfixt

"The grace for which I prayed; and now
The death-damp gathers on my brow,
But to God's will I cannot bow.

"O, I would live! I dread this death,
This sudden sinking of the breath,
With all the mystery beneath;

"With all the fear beyond the pain,
With all the mist beyond the rain—
O God! O Christ! I would remain!"

She lieth dead—the church-bells toll—
Fair Father Christ, receive her soul
And make the broken image whole.

Etchings.

Etchings.

CASSIUS.

ERECT!—with strained nerves list'ning to
the blare
Of Cæsar's trumpets—from his strong
grasp slips
A world of empire—brow, and chin, and
lips
Knit in a grim half-frown, half-sneer—despair

Pants in his breath. Above the trodden plain
The golden eagles leer and onward press;
As one that seeketh freedom from duress
His bloodshot eyes roll right and left, in vain,

But with a somber joy grow fixed to greet
The dinted steel, dull red with battle-rust,
And, at the bidding of the warrior's thrust,
Light, Night, and Death on swart Philippi meet.

A RAINY DAY IN TOWN.

RAIN, rain, and rain! all day the ceaseless patter
Makes the streets moist and dim—the dampened smoke
Hangs in the air—the buildings reek and soak—
Bedraggled horses trot with splash and clatter—
The wet pedestrians tread a yellow batter
Out of the mud—old women cough and choke—
Young women with umbrellas push and poke,

And wretched fog makes worse the dismal
matter.
So down a dirty tide the dull day floats
Till evening with no friendly hand spreads
out
A shivering darkness—work-girls hurry
by
With poor thin shawls pinned tight about
their throats—
The street-lamps blearing thro' the rainy
rout,
Each like a winking, sickly evil-eye.

THE SENTINEL.

THE midnight moon behind the forest trees
Slow-moving, cowled in fleecy mist and cloud,
The poplars rustled by the passing breeze,
The sleepless spiders spinning shroud on shroud.

The frowning turrets and the arch of stone,
The great gate barred, with massive bolt across,
The upraised drawbridge, and the sullen moan
Of sluggish waters in the open fosse.

A gleam of light—and, on his lonely round,
With lantern at his belt, and levied spear,
Whistling a summons to his laggard hound,
With stride and strut goes by the halberdier.

ORPHEUS.

A LEVEL stretch of turnpike, winding round
Thro' pasturelands and fields of waving grain
Fresh-blown with perfume of the April rain—
A little grove—and, stretched upon the ground,

A way-worn tinker, lolling at his ease
Beneath an elm, and trolling out his song—
An old romaunt—in mellow voice, and strong,
While thrush and blackbird, flitting from the trees,

Perch on his head, and chatter round his
feet,
And feast on crumbs from out his friendly
hand,
And sing in rivalry, till thro' the land
The chorus swells, melodiously sweet.

L'ENFANT TERRIBLE.

A RUINED keep, with rusty gate
Creaking below a broken arch,
The forest heavy with the weight
Of rugged pine and clustered larch.

A shout! a leap! and mounted on
The wind-blown gate, with white head bare,
An urchin sits, and whoops anon
Till frolic echoes shake the air.

With swinging legs he madly rides,
Both hands above his head held fast;
The huge red sun behind him slides
And shapes a shadow long and vast.

Personal Tributes.

Personal Tributes.

TO CLARA MORRIS.

(After seeing "Alixe.")

FRESH as the winds of morn upon the sea,
Fair as the first red rose of joyous June,
Pure as a white cloud blown across the moon
When summer nights glow soft on hill and lea—

How shall I fitly yield my praise to thee?
For thine the subtle charm no rhyme or rune
Can shadow forth, nor music set to tune;
Lo, thou beyond all reach of art dost flee;
With silver chime of happy girlish mirth,
With lambent virgin eyes that open up
To Love, as violets to the winter sun—
And O, when comes the cruel curse of earth
Thy firm young lips drain dry the bitter cup—
Yes, blood of martyrs in thy veins doth run.

TO ALFRED TENNYSON.

O THOU that wear'st so well the poet's wreath,
Behold thy songs flown hither o'er the seas
To make unto our souls sweet melodies,
To show the truth and love that lie beneath
All things—men's hearts, or brambles of the heath,
Or rolling stars, or dim immensities—
The spirit of thy song strikes light from these,
A sword of flame drawn from a starry sheath.

And when the deep'ning shadows shall have
rolled
O'er this our age, on dusty winds upborne,
Still shall men speak of thee with loving
stress ;
Tho' many sounds be hushed in that gray fold,
Still thro' the years shall wind the silver
horn
Blown from the sea-girt walls of Lyonesse.

TO ALGERNON CHARLES SWINBURNE.

LORD of the lyre! of languaged lightning lord!
Master of matchless, melting melody!
Phosphor of Freedom! foe of falsity!
Smiter of sin with song's swift, sleepless sword!—
Lo, tyrants tremble as they turn toward
Thee, pearled and panoplied in poesy,
Winged for the warfield, waiting wistfully
Thy ripe Republic of all rights restored.

Not vain thy voice! lo, vague and vilified,
Divine Democracy draws near, discerned
Of hinds and heroes, halting yet, half-
turned
To watch this West, whence, wonderful and
wide,
Flashes the flame of Freedom's firmament,
Crowning our crownless, kingless conti-
nent.

TO FRANK MAYO.

DEAR friend and brother—brother by more than blood,
By the close ties of mind, the bonds of soul,
Whereby we know us atoms of one whole,
Twin drops in the immeasurable flood;
In thee I love to watch the blossoming bud
Of thought, that, slow of growth as bedded coal,
Developed points to truth's far-flaming goal
And shows to others the way from mire and mud.

Not for thy matchless, masterful player's art,
With which thou mak'st me laugh or weep at will,
Do I my full affection render thee;
Nay, rather for thy loyal, noble heart,
Thy brave, true manhood, that among us still
Keeps fresh the flower and fruit of chivalry.

TO WILLIAM YOUNG.

BELOVED comrade in the gracious art
Of rhyme and song, what shall I say to thee?
Save as some brooklet, purling nigh the sea,
Sings to the sea in wonder-stricken start:
"O, vast and strong! O, passionate of heart!
That hast the knowledge of much mystery!
Thou sufferest for thy very majesty,
In that forever thou must dwell apart.

Yet in thy loneliness is compensation,
For thou art filled with limitless, sweet light,
And in thy storms lurk poignant ecstacies;
Up to the sun life-giving exhalation
Thou flingest, and the amorous moon at night
Disturbs thy breast with ardent vagaries."

TO E. B.

O FAIR it is to see some mighty oak
Lording the forest with his great green crown,
And fair to see, above the clustered town,
The towered fort that shields from foreign yoke ;
But fairer yet, creation's masterstroke,
A strong, brave man, who scorns the fret and frown
Of Fortune—one who looks not back nor down
But stands high-hearted, firm amid his folk.

A type of our great race, persistent, loyal,
Ready to dare and do in Right's defence,
Or bear such work-day toil as heroes can;
In loving, steadfast; and in giving, royal—
Even so, my friend, in thee I reverence
A stalwart, sovereign, self-swayed, Saxon
man.

The Human Quest.

PRELUDE

WHO may find
What the wind
        Bloweth down the hollow?
Who may hear
Words of cheer
        Sunless silence follow?

Who can say
How To-day
        Shall become To-morrow?

Who can say
Yesterday
        Did not die in sorrow?

Who can tell
When the knell
        Shall be ringing for him?
Who would dream
With the gleam
        Of unknown stars o'er him?

Round and round,
Void of sound,
        Floats the Holy Vision—
Floats, departs,
And our hearts
        Find alone derision.

I.

DESPAIR.

FULL many a time the poet strikes his lyre
To hear therefrom no sweet, responsive thrill;
Often the painter, toiling, fails to fill
The parted lips with life, the eyes with fire;
Days come too when the sculptor's strong hands tire
Because they may not work his marble will—
Yea, all men know the hour when hope lies still
And the sad soul aches with a dumb desire.

Wan moments!—then the gray marge of the
world
Dips to an utter emptiness, where all
Lies hid beneath the impenetrable pall;
Man and his earth but helpless nothings,
hurled
By luckless chance along an aimless
path,
Too small for power and too weak for
wrath.

II.

AFAR!

AFAR, afar, the shining hill-tops rise;
 So far the stars at dawn sink into them
 And leave the round moon lonely on the hem
Of night that fades—ah, ye with straining eyes
And eager hands, wherefore in any wise
 Can ye have hope to climb aloft and stem
 The rush of streams that flow but to condemn?
So far, so far, the hill-tops fret the skies.

And eyes wax dim with searching for the way,
Strong hands grow weak from vain desire and prayer,
The ruddy gold of youth turns ashen-gray
But still goes on the never ending quest,
Even as the wind that moves the upper air
Blows ever from the regions of the west.

III.

IMPERFECTION.

THERE came a sudden brightness in the night,
Above the world uprose an awful flame
That hid within its heart the secret name;
Before all men it leaped from height to height!
A clear voice broke the stillness of affright,
Saying: "The perfect one devoid of blame
Shall read the scroll within this fiery frame,
And God be plainly known as noon-tide light."

Then all men watched the flame with eager
eyes
And souls beat at the eyeballs follow-
ing it
As birds wear out their wings against
the bars;
But, lo, the hours sped on, and thro' the skies
The white flame passed and left the
world unlit
Save for the far dim light of distant
stars.

IV.

IF.

IF that white light should shine from very far
And show God's face all wet with piteous tears,
And men should look thereon and lose their fears,
And faith grow strong, and clear as yonder star—
What then 'twixt God and man could be a bar?
What sharp unrest make sad the rapid years?
As they are made to him who sees and hears
But frail faint phantoms of the things that are.

In truth, tho' man should see his very God,
His soul would suffer that the last were known;
And he, found powerless as any thrall,
Would still curse laws that bound him to this sod
With wit and will to scale the utmost throne,
But with no strength or power to more than crawl.

V.

DISCONTENT.

SAITH Atlas: "On me rest the pillars of heaven,
Always I bend beneath the weary load,
Always I tread the endless, circling road
That runs from night to noon, from noon to even—
But in my blood still glows the living leaven
That filled me when from peak to peak I strode,
Rocks in my hands, straight up to God's abode
And waged a war that left His mountains riven.

So terrible a battle-blast did blow
All Heaven reeled and leaned toward outer space;
Then lightnings flashed from the omnipotent face
And with a sign He set me here below."
Is this the prop to uphold a firmament,
Broad-backed defeat and sinewy discontent?

VI.

A DREAM.

ONE night it grew so still upon the earth
That I could hear the planets on their march,
Lo, suddenly the sombre midnight arch
Transparent grew through all its mighty girth—
Ah, then the giant splendor was beholden
Of God's domain; all glorious stars were seen
Parts of one august whole; a light serene
Shone from the deeps most luminously golden.

Swiftly and sweetly that great light increased,
I whispered: "God is coming from on high!"—
But as I spake the light was shut away;
And from the darkened, dreamy, violet east,
With brandished spears uplifted to the sky,
Came forth the golden heralds of the day.

VII.

HOPE.

O FAINT of heart take courage!—all is dark,
Yet all is light—we know not but we feel!
We cannot see where whirls the central wheel
And yet the ever-moving stars we mark.
O Hope sublime! thou art a very ark
Wherein to rest, to dream, perchance to kneel,
And in sweet visions see the sights that heal
And hear the sounds—all senses crying: "Hark!"

Yea, visible law and love from while to while
Smite this far orb with their unerring rod,
On Saint Helena shone no august smile,
Earth's slayer crumbled into earth's own sod;
But he of Patmos from his barren isle
Saw things to blind one—yea, and talked with God.

VIII.

AD ASTRA.

1.

O DOUBT that runs thro' every mood!
O hope that comes to souls who brood!
O tender, sad disquietude!

Shall peace at any time be found,
Or knowledge make a perfect round
Where now is neither sight nor sound?

Men ask in vain of creeds and schools,
The holy fire of vision cools,
Quenched in their unrelenting rules.

They say: "His laws are not our laws,
He doeth naught without a cause,
Where reason stops we cry you 'pause!'"

But leaf and bud and sea and star
Call out from near, call out from far,—
"Behold, in reason all things are!"

In reason, law, that governs all,
That makes the ripened apple fall,
Or whirls a planet like a ball.

2.

Behold the grand similitude
That human knowledge, yet so crude,
Finds, marvellous and many-hued.

The unity that swells and rings
To harmony, wherein God sings
The oneness of existing things.

Where'er the lines of truth expand
We find the same all-shaping hand
Strong with the same divine command.

The law that makes the red ant creep,
Or little chirping crickets leap,
Rolls stars along the midnight deep.

The light that shines from yonder sphere
Is one with that which flickers here
From candle set at font or bier.

The foam at dawn that flecks the main,
The flowers that gem the summer plain,
The rainbow poised 'twixt sky and rain,

With the same seven colors glow,
The seven hues that blend and show
The perfect whiteness of the snow.

Worlds roll round suns, and they in turn
Roll round some mightier orbs, that burn
In vaster space than we discern.

Far reaching laws! from sward to sky
Embracing all things, low and high,
In wide, sublime analogy.

3

O in this unity of all
As one must be the things we call
Material and spiritual.

No false division-wall would rise
If one could look with flesh-free eyes
Thro' all these somber mysteries.

The universe but thought made clear—
Soul-flesh, flesh-soul twin truths appear—
But, ah, thro' silence thrills the fear,

The fear we only half resist
That all is but a dream, a mist,
A fancy of the egotist.

4

Must we forever be half-blind?
Shall we forever fail to find
The answer?—Nay, O human mind,

Courage!—thy path is upward! lo,
On loftiest peaks abides the snow
And loftiest flights are cold and slow.

But haply now the day is nigh
When every orb that rolls on high
Shall smile a message from the sky;

When, to the august strains that roll
From sea to sea, from pole to pole,—
All sound in one great hymn made whole—

Some mighty soul shall wave a wand,
And, piercing thro' the starry frond,
Reveal the Unknown God beyond.

THE END.

www.ingramcontent.com/pod-product-compliance
Lightning Source LLC
LaVergne TN
LVHW011219110826
845150LV00006B/1477